BOOK REVIEWS

A Woman's Story (Her Prerogative Spoken Through His Words) By Derrick Graham is a journey through the life and heart of a woman at various points in her life as she sometimes smiles and sometimes struggles to make sense of the world and her situation in it.

The poems are written in the first person by the woman (in whose voice Derrick Graham is speaking) The book, that is almost like a diary of a woman, is a good mix of poems of gravity, and those in a lighter vein. Some talk of incidents, some of feelings and others of her own shortcomings, as she sees them.

What stands out is the poetic introduction and ending to the book where the poet speaks to the reader in a poem.

The poetry here spills the words hidden in the heart of a woman, as a man sees it, and that makes them different from the other books where the man or the woman is speaking for himself or herself.

Some of the parts that I found very appealing are

Until you become a mother
You won't know what they've been through (from Being A Good Mother)

You don't appreciate a good thing
Until it finally leaves you (from Good Thing)

When I write a poem
They always seem to rhyme

and

When I write a poem
My mind and soul are free
It allows for more familiarization
For myself to get to know me (from When I Write a Poem)

I Return the Favor is a particularly touching piece for its feelings.

If you are looking for poetry with a simplicity of language, an inspiring, conversational tone and feelings that many women will identify with, read this very nicely put-together collection from Derrick Graham.

"This book is a must read. The reader is taken though the stages following heart break, pain and triumph by beautifully written poems. Each poem holds the reader's attention and lure him to the next as he gets more and more invested in the emotional twist and turns of the author's experiences. The poems are raw and each word is a genuine piece of the author for the reader to experience and identify with. I can't recommend this book enough. It has taken me on a healing journey, I didn't know I needed."

-editor of URLINK-

"This is such a great book. I've been down for a while now and poetry always makes me feel better about the way I feel and this book is so amazing. Derrick does wonders with words and makes you feel them to your core. Definitely recommend this book to anyone. I can't wait to purchase his next one."

-reviewer of URLINK-

A WOMAN'S STORY

Her Prerogative Spoken Through His Words

A WOMAN'S STORY

DERRICK GRAHAM

A Woman's Story

Copyright © 2019 by Derrick Graham. All rights reserved.

No part of this publication may be reproduced, stored in a retrieval system or transmitted in any way by any means, electronic, mechanical, photocopy, recording or otherwise without the prior permission of the author except as provided by USA copyright law.

The opinions expressed by the author are not necessarily those of URLink Print and Media.

1603 Capitol Ave., Suite 310 Cheyenne, Wyoming USA 82001
1-888-980-6523 | admin@urlinkpublishing.com

URLink Print and Media is committed to excellence in the publishing industry.

Book design copyright © 2019 by URLink Print and Media. All rights reserved.

Published in the United States of America
ISBN 978-1-64367-773-6 (Paperback)
ISBN 978-1-64367-772-9 (Digital)

15.08.19

ACKNOWLEDGEMENT

I would like to thank the Lord for blessing me once more for the positive influences in my life. My wife, Felesha, has always been there for me which has made such a difference in helping develop my creativity.

    I would also like to thank the following individuals who have made this possible. My mother Lois Graham, Jo Anita Miley, Velvet Holden, and my family which have influenced me through my life's journey, I thank you all.

CONTENTS

Inspirational

Being a Good Mother 1
Continue To Rise 2
An Aspect of Love 4
In Everything I Do 5
No Disrespect 6
Good Thing 7
Leave 9
What If 11
Essence of a Woman 13
When I Write a Poem 14
Just For Me 16
My Senses 17
Thank You Mom 18
Special Love 20
For You 22
Woman's Intuition 23
Don't Doubt Me 25
I Return the Favor 26

Spiritual

Each Day 28
Lord Help Me 29
Talk To You 30

Sensual

My Sexy Man 32
I Choose You 33
It Happens Every Time 34
The Morning After 35
Body Language 36
My Heart Says Yes 37
Comeback 38
In His Eyes 39
One Sad Day 40
Black Out 42
Tragic Story 44
Just Don't Lie 45
Love Is 47
One Heart to Give 49
Dear Diary 51
Me and You 53
Woman's Prerogative 55
A Night Out 56
That Guy 57
Sometimes 59

General

Beginning of a Storm 60
Butterfly 61
Women Role Models 63
Dear Daughter 64
Battered Woman 65
We Need a Resolution 66
Dinner for Two 67
Her Time 68
Not My Type 69
Based On Your Lies 70
Warning Signs 71

The End	73
Every Life Matters	74
Stay True	76
Military Mothers	77
The Game	79
The Thought Process	80
Freedom	81
I Thank You	84

Being a Good Mother

This book has been dedicated
To all the women around the world
Who have sacrificed and struggled
In raising the children of the world

To ensure that they are safe
And each day they're fed
To teach them what is right
At night tuck them into bed

For the women who have cried
For those who've stressed alone
For those very same women
Turned their house into a home

The children may not know
How these things came to be?
Somethings they don't need to know
And others they need to see

As you continue to read on
Remember this to be true
Until you become a mother
You won't know what they've been through

Continue To Rise

When you're at the bottom
Trying to climb to the top
No matter how challenging it is
You must never stop

There will be distractions
And pitfalls along the way
There'll be forked tongued serpents
Having something to say

They'll try to mislead you
They don't want you to see
The potential that you have
And all what you could be

They will try to deceive you
Telling convincing lies
But you know much better
As you continue to rise

Though you get very tired
And frustrated at what they say
You must continue to climb
Making progress each day

Sometimes you may slip
After so many tries
But you must never stop
As you continue to rise

An Aspect of Love

The heart is an organ
That's often thought of
As a place for emotions
To develop into love

These feelings are an attachment
An abstract in the mind
That longs for attention
And desires quality time

It also requires love
To be given and returned
A natural human behavior
That's appreciated and learned

Its strength is boundless
And fortified by chains
It can break men down
And do women the same

It can make you submissive
And so crazy in love
It weighs heavy on the heart
That's the meaning of love

In Everything I Do

I strive to be better
In everything I do
It should be evident in my actions
My dedication is true

When everything seems perfect
I listen to my heart
My actions will be understood
That's how it usually starts

But when things go wrong
With a cloud over my head
I stop to think back
Was it something I said?

Was it something I've done?
What did I do wrong?
Tell me so I may correct it
And then I can move on

I refuse to be a burden
Or carry one around
My life is stressful enough
Without something else pulling me down

No Disrespect

If love isn't the issue
And if it's not about us
Then it must be about me
Am I not enough?

I had a strong feeling
It was just a matter of time
I felt he wanted to leave
The thought had crossed my mind

I knew what was going on
But I didn't say a word
I never did confront him
With all the things I heard

I never believed in rumors
But what I've always believed
If there was ever a problem
Then he should talk to me

This is how I think
He knew this when we met
I can take a lot of things
But I won't deal with disrespect

Good Thing

You know that I'm leaving
And this is how it should be
I am confident when I say this
You won't find anyone like me

I put up with so much
What's the use in trying?
All you do is keep dogging me
With your infidelity and lying

I'm tired of you walking out
And saying you're going to leave
I've beginning to realize
You're not the right one for me

I know what needs to happen
It came to me the other day
I know someone had to leave
I know it was happening today

I had so many plans for us
But all you did was lie
This is why we become violent
Do you really have to ask why

If you can't understand this
Then what they say is true
You don't appreciate a good thing
Until it finally leaves you

Leave

I often close my eyes
When I count to three
Taking a deep breath
That often works for me

I do this when I'm alone
To calm down from the strife
From all the twist and turns
I've dealt with in my life

I get up and walk around
But in the mirror I can see
The brutal marks he left
When he put his hands on me

As I stare at my reflection
Looking over my bruised face
Filled with anger and resentment
Covered in disgrace

What did I do wrong?
Is this really about me?
Is this how my life?
Is really supposed to be?

It's not as easy as they think
But I truly do believe
The Lord gave me enough strength
To pack my bags and leave

What If

What if I gave you my heart?
What would you do?
Would you protect it from harm?
Would you throw that away too?

Would you think about the damage?
Since you treated me this way
Would you have a good explanation?
What could you possibly say?

You keep ignoring the facts
I know you can see
You're not accepting of your faults
All you do is blame me

I've done all I can
What more can I do
How dare you treat me this way
What if I did this to you

You've made it so obvious
I'm not what you need
You have a ravenous appetite
Consumed by such greed

But remember the saying
Because karma is so true
How would you feel
If I did the same to you

Essence of a Woman

I am strong and liberated
And difficult to understand
I am determined in my agenda
No different than a man

If I see something I want
I'll watch then I'll see
If he is definitely the man
That's perfect for me

And if he's not, that's fine
Then we'll just be friends
And not with any benefits
I won't do that again

I'm speaking of my heart
My mind and my soul
I don't need to give a reason
I have already said no

They can say what they want
I won't change my mind
It's better for you to move on
And stop wasting your time

When I Write a Poem

When I write a poem
They always seem to rhyme
I don't plan it that way
It's the thoughts that cross my mind

As I transcribe these thoughts
From nothing to something real
When the words hit the page
They're emotions I can feel

Sometimes I loose myself
In the descriptive words I use
I'm just trying to relay a message
Of my experiences to you

When I write a poem
My mind and soul are free
It allows for more familiarization
For myself to get to know me

It helps me to reminisce
About the things I've been through
It requires me to be established
In everything I do

The best thing about it all
It has helped me to find
Something that I've longed for
That's a peace of mind

Just For Me

I want to be noticed
Not only for what you see
I want to be loved and cherished
But only just for me

I will give you my all
That's faithful and true
I will love unconditionally
But only just for you

As we make sacrifices
To be with each other
Then our hearts will unite
And together form another

Because I am for you
And you're there for me
This is how our life
Is really supposed to be

My Senses

My eyes have shed many tears
They've also seen many deaths
They've witnessed the birth of a newborn
Taking its very first breath

My ears have heard many things
I really don't care to share
The situation became so bad
Even I wished I wasn't there

My mind has often taught me
The differences in what I think
And not to voice those differences
Sometimes it's better not to speak

My heart continues to love
Despite what I've been through
But I don't easily get discourage
This is how I met you

Thank You Mom

I'm inspired by many things
But the closest to my soul
The things the Lord has given me
Since I was one day old

I didn't know what I had
Or how special it could be
But as I became older
It became obvious to me

We've spent so much time together
Throughout all these years
We've shared happy moments
And endured some painful tears

I remember so many things
How you'd protect me from harm
The only safe place for me
Was being comforted in your arms

You never did complain
You became my best friend
And if I had the chance
I would do it all again

You put up with so much
And all my childish ways
Thank you for your patience
For all those memorable days

Special Love

Love can mean many things
It can also be something to give
It can be a vital part of your life
It's something you must have to live

To want something so bad
To want great passion and desire
To have the love of your life
To fuel your eternal fire

Love can mean something special
To be patient in every way
To hang on to their last word
To listen to what they say

Be mindful of their thoughts
To understand how they feel
To be gentle in your approach
To have a love that's real

Love with all your heart
And from the depths of your soul
Allow the passion to take over
Let the desire take control

Thank you for your patience
By not treating me any less
Thanks for loving me forever
And giving me your very best

For You

I always try to be thoughtful
And careful in what I do
I want you to understand
I would do anything for you

I wish I could truly explain
But I'm sure you already know
I've tried to express it in words
That's about as far as it goes

Sometimes it's kind of difficult
For me to get you to see
How much I really love you
And what you mean to me

You're inside my heart and mind
Literally, I wish you were there
So you could see for yourself
How much I do care

This is how deeply I love
It sounds crazy but it's true
My heartfelt emotions
Are only reserved for you

Woman's Intuition

You want to wine me and dine me
You want to sweep me off my feet
You want me to give you my all
At least that's what you want me to think

But my woman's intuition
Is really strong this time
It's telling me to be cautious
Because this man is not mine

That means I'm not important
No matter what he said
He wants me to believe every word
He's trying to put inside my head

I've heard it all before
But what he doesn't know
I could have been that woman
Not too long ago

I tried to overlook it
I acknowledged the warning signs
I've done all the research
I've read every line

Please understand the game
And watch what they do
Because the game could be reversed
Now who's playing who?

Don't Doubt Me

I remembered what you said
I wouldn't make it without you
You're a bigger fool than I thought
If you believe that to be true

You think that you know me
But you really don't
You think that I would fail
But you know that I won't

Don't tell me that I can't
Because you know that I will
I'm better off without you
This time it's for real

I didn't really need you
Why was it so hard to believe?
I always handle my business
You shouldn't have doubted me

I Return the Favor

She has always been accurate
She'd really didn't have a flaw
I lived by her rules
Which she called the law

At times it was rough
But I knew she cared
It wasn't easy for her
Still she was always there

I remembered all those times
We were there for each other
Now it's my turn
To take care of my mother

Her memory is not the same
It appears to be getting worse
Strong signs of dementia
Has begun to take its course

It hurts me to see her like this
When there's nothing I can do
To help ease this painful moment
We both are going through

I love her with all my heart
She's always been there for me
I will continue to stay with her
There's no place I rather be

Each Day

Each day that I awake
I must not forget to say
Thank you my dear Lord
For allowing me another day

I will do my very best
To appreciate what I have
And I must never forget
To take time out to laugh

At times I may feel bad
Not everyone needs to know
The remedy takes sometime
As the course is often slow

I must continue to be diligent
Because, this is what I do
Life is so unpredictable
This is nothing new

My faith is solidified
And this is why I say
Thank you my dear Lord
For giving me this day

Lord Help Me

I want to thank you Lord
For all my fruitful days
For loving and caring for me
Even when I had strayed

For keeping the door open
With you arms extended wide
For placing food on my table
And dining by my side

For providing me with a bed
And a blanket to fight the cold
For giving me your love
To a poor confused soul

For showing me the way
When my selfish eyes couldn't see
For continuously giving me guidance
While providing a way for me

For all the times you directed me
And watched over me each day
For the obstacles I've overcame
Because you made a way

Talk To You

Lord I need to talk to you
I need your help somehow
I've been feeling quite depressed
For more than a year now

I don't know how it started
But I know how it could end
I'm afraid of having a relapse
And reliving that moment again

I haven't told anybody
There's nothing they can do
They don't love me unconditionally
They don't care for me like you

As I get down on my knees
And tears roll down my face
I feel so desperately alone
In a not-so friendly place

As I continue to pray
My mind drifts a little more
My tears flow more freely
More so than before

I want to thank you Lord
For your enormous sacrifice
By giving your only son
In order to save my life

Amen

My Sexy Man

He has dark colored eyes
And really smooth skin
A caramel complexion
He's my perfect ten

He's about six feet tall
With a pair of sexy lips
They are ideal for kissing
And caressing my hips

His arms are muscular
His chest so defined
His feet are kind of large
This is a good sign

His cologne is captivating
His lips are so soft
As I fantasize of pleasure
This really gets my off

I motion him to come closer
As I gently close my eyes
I slowly guide his head down
To get a special surprise

I Choose You

We've been through so much
And yet we still stand
Like on our wedding day
Your hand inside my hand

Whatever problems we faced
We've always done it together
As we continue this journey
It's you and me forever

We've had some good times
And some passionate moments too
Walking down the aisle
To spend my life with you

I still feel the same way
And I must confess
My love is always yours
My heart still says yes

We belong together
Because I choose you
In the present and the future
And in everything I do

It Happens Every Time

When you kiss me gently
A sensation runs down my spine
It travels throughout my body
It happens every time

It's a spontaneous feeling
Its intensity is always the same
It's like an insatiable desire
Calling out my name

When you touch me all over
The feeling is revived
I can't control this emotion
It happens every time

It overwhelms me to think
I have that guy, so it seems
The one they said didn't exist
The one that's in my dreams

I understand this feeling
Filled with a love that's so true
It happens every time
But only when I'm with you

The Morning After

Last night was phenomenal
I had a lovely time
I've got the strangest feeling
There's something on your mind

I can tell how you're acting
You can't look me in the eye
You're avoiding the issue
I'm curious to know why

He looked at her and said
I had a wonderful time too
I love it when we're together
When it's just me and you

I know you can tell
When something's on my mind
But there's nothing wrong
I was waiting for the right time

He gently takes her hand
And slowly got on one knee
He looked her in the eyes
And ask would you marry me?

Body Language

Listening can be difficult
For someone to embrace
Especially if they're shy
And can't look you in the face

It may appear they don't talk
The body is saying something else
You have to pay close attention
To notice it for yourself

Body language is an alternative
To be seen instead of heard
That translates so many actions
Simply into words

But sometimes there are times
Where words are not preferred
Then body chemistry takes over
To say much more than words

The connection is so evident
As they communicate that way
Body language still speaks louder
Than words could ever say

My Heart Says Yes

Just sitting here thinking
As I have a glass of wine
Reminiscing on how we met
Thinking back on those times

I was trying to be cautious
I was reluctant to let you in
My heart's been broken before
And I won't let it happen again

No matter how difficult I was
You were able to get through
You made it so very easy
To fall in love with you

At that moment everything changed
You told me you would be honest
No matter how difficult it may be
You've always kept your promise

There have been upsetting moments
When I wasn't always right
You listened to me unconditionally
And comforted me at night

Comeback

Since the day you left me
I've been all alone
It really broke my heart
To know that you're gone

And all I can do is think
Most of the time I'm sad
It never really dawned on me
What I really had

I wish I could change it
I never wanted it to end
I admit I made a mistake
Can we start over again?

But I don't think that's possible
You gave me back my key
I feel I'm the last person
In the world you want to see

You wouldn't feel this way
If your love wasn't true
I know you're hurting inside
I feel the same as you

In His Eyes

When I look into his eyes
I only see him and me
A life which we planned
That's how we wanted to be

But I know much more
Then he thinks that I know
Although he doesn't suspect it
His eyes have told me so

You see, I understand him
And I listen to him too
I hear what he has to say
I know what he's going through

When he comes home from work
I give him time to unwind
To get settled inside our home
To tell me what's on his mind

When I look into his eyes
I can also see the pain
How much he struggles?
For him, I do the same

One Sad Day

She wasn't that popular
When she was in high school
She was thought of as a nerd
She abide by the rules

She didn't go to many parties
She kept her head in the books
She often worked hard at it
Not matter how long it took

She wanted to be a police officer
It was something she loved
That's all she ever talked about
The only thing she thought of

She got accepted to the academy
She was so excited that day
Especially when she graduated
That was her special day

When she got to her new unit
She was patrolling the neighborhood
Making her presence known
As a new police officer should

As she got out of her vehicle
Multiple shots rang out
People started running everywhere
As they screamed and shout

She was transported to the hospital
But somehow along the way
She expired while in transport
It was one of the saddest days

Black Out

My friends have often told me
About my actions at times
When I get really angry
I seem to lose my mind

One day we were talking
And things became intense
My mind began to drift off
That's when I clinched my fists

I didn't realize what I was doing
Everything happened so fast
Reminiscing on bad experiences
I had encountered in the past

They were trying to talk me down
I didn't know what about
The conversation was confusing
It appeared I had blacked out

In other words, I was here
But my mind was somewhere else
Isolated from the entire world
And at times, including myself

I finally discovered the trigger
The primary cause of this mess
I understand the problem now
I can't handle too much stress

Tragic Story

It hurts with great sadness
To hear someone say
We're sorry for your loss
When a loved one's passed away

No words can quite describe
The agony and the pain
The coping of the struggle
Including all the strain

Sometimes it's so hard
Just too really comprehend
As you fight back the tears
Reliving the moment again

Denial drives the emotions
Not to accept what is real
Acceptance is the reality
Of what you truly feel

As life brings new obstacles
In everything you do
You have to be prepared
And embrace the changes too

Just Don't Lie

You know it's kind of funny
How you befriended me
It's the way you introduced yourself
It made me feel sort of edgy

My inquisitive suspicions
Were getting the best of me
Learning from past experiences
Was something I had to believe

It's not a preconceived notion
Let's just call it a gut check
To always be on the look out
For that guy I haven't met

Even though I'm on guard
I'll see what he's about
I don't think it will take too long
To really figure him out

I want to know his intentions
Is he playing a childish game?
Utilizing misleading propaganda
In hopes of uplifting his name

That's why so many women
Do the things they do
Because of all the bad things
Rotten men have put them through

Love Is

Love is immensely boundless
That brings so much joy
Filled with vigorous energy
Which could never be destroyed?

Fueled with such a force
It could deliver a massive blow
That could obliterate any heart
If it were ever to explode

Love is so forgiving
But it does take some time
To excuse unwanted behavior
Within the soul and mind

Patience is an extension
What love is supposed to be?
It can be difficult to acquire
Especially for me

Love is very comforting
When you feel alone
It can change any heart
Even if it's made of stone

This emotion is spontaneous
It can sometimes leave a scar
But love is always the same
No matter where you are

One Heart to Give

Do you remember what I said?
I don't want to fall in love
That emotion no longer exist
It's the last thing I'm thinking of

I've given up on that feeling
It doesn't live here anymore
How many times must I say it?
So I'll tell you this once more

When I became involved
I enjoyed the life we lived
I told you from the start
I have one heart to give

I needed you to protect it
And guard it with your life
Cherish every moment
As if I were your wife

For a while you did that
You made me feel alive
You gave love a new meaning
My heart felt so revived

You suddenly began to change
Then a thought crossed my mind
You were sending me a message
I can see the warning signs

Dear Diary

I've cried all night long
I couldn't fight back the tears
I just recently found out
I've been lied to all these years

He didn't have to do this
He should've talked to me
We could've worked this out
And somehow come to agree

But instead he wanted to play
I guess he thought it was fun
He should've thought about this
Believe me, I'm not the one

I cried, not because I'm hurt
But in fear of what I'll do
My anger isn't so forgiving
Especially when it comes to you

I told him how I was
I even gave him an out
I told him I don't play games
He knew what I was about

Since he thought this was a joke
It's time I've have some fun
Remember you started this mess
Now the games have just begun

Me and You

I know we need to talk
It's a hard thing to do
There's something you need to know
About me and you

I can sense something different
I can see it on your face
You need some time alone
I know you need your space

Although, I didn't like it
I really must agree
It's the only way that things
Could be better between you and me

Through all of the thinking
Through all of the crying
Through all of the sleepless nights
Inside I've been dying

My emotions are fragile
And should be handled with care
These feelings won't stop
But I will always be there

I want you to know
That I need you too
We have to make better decisions
If we are going to make it through

Woman's Prerogative

I have made a choice
Sometimes it's hard to choose
I've always wanted to be a winner
But sometimes in life you lose

Life is so unpredictable
You'll never know each day
It's difficult remaining focused
And ignoring what people say

But since it's my prerogative
It doesn't matter what others do
Because I know in my heart
I will always remain true

A Night Out

She's finally off work
And it's the weekend
It's time to turn up
Going out with some friends

She's just took a shower
And finished curling her hair
Thinking of where to go
And what she's going to wear

She picks out a sexy dress
With some cute high-heel shoes
She has a lot of options
It's difficult to choose

She grabs her cell phone
To get her girls on the line
It's a quarter to eleven
It's about that time

That Guy

I said I wasn't getting married
And I wasn't falling in love
I have yet to meet the man
That I've always dreamed of

My friends and co-workers
Said my standards are set too high
They said there's no way in the world
I would ever find that guy

I refused to believe them
When my heart says yes
Because I had settled for someone
That always kept me stressed

But I never gave up
Then again, I didn't try
I was really beginning to think
There was no such guy

Until one day it happened
It was such a wonderful surprise
I knew he was the one
When I looked into his eyes

My prayers have been answered
My dreams had finally come true
They say you didn't exist
Now I know better, because I have you

Sometimes

Sometimes I feel like crying
Just like the pouring rain
But my heart won't allow me
Being traumatized by the pain

It builds up inside me
Like air in a small balloon
It won't be long now
Before I explode soon

Sometimes I feel alone
Isolated in a large cage
My heart often feels no love
In this depressed stage

Like a tree with no water
And a flower with no sun
Life is diminishing fast
When it should only just begun

Even though I can't cry
And I don't know why
The feeling still lingers
But sometimes I still try

Beginning of a Storm

As the dark clouds move in
They block out the sun's rays
The temperature hasn't changed
It looks like one of those days

Heavier clouds join the formation
Bringing much of the same
Then the thunder begins clapping
But still no sign of rain

The wind becomes much stronger
And the trees begin to sway
A glimpse of lightening is seen
As it brightens this darken day

The leaves are blowing everywhere
The thunder is getting loud
The lightening is getting much closer
As no one makes a sound

Debris hits the house
As the temperature begins to change
It finally begins to sprinkle
The very first signs of rain

Butterfly

I once saw a small butterfly
Motionless on the dry concrete
I was fascinated with its colors
As it laid calmly by my feet

It was mostly black
With some shades of blue
It appeared to be resting
Peacefully, but it won't move

I started to it pick up
Then I changed my mind
It's lying there for a reason
I'll just give it some time

I didn't want to disturb it
It might had another plan
One that didn't concern me
Not that I'd understand

But when I came back
To that spot that day
The butterfly was gone
I guess it finally flew away

With such beautiful colors
A wonderful site to see
A picture perfect moment
That often relaxes me

Women Role Models

It's evident around the world
No matter where you go
The contributions they've made
The important positions they hold

They own their own businesses
They are professional athletes
They are brave police officers
That patrol and protect our streets

They are courageous servicewomen
That are devoted in what they do
They deployed to foreign lands
Protecting the country for me and you

And don't forget the reporters
Those are reporting in harm's way
Sacrificing their safety
To report the news each day

These are their contributions
Influences they're willing to give
For a more prosperous future
For all our children to live

Dear Daughter

Ever since you were born
I took good care of you
I watched over you closely
Just as all mothers do

And when you started talking
You would often repeat words
You didn't know what they mean
It was things you overheard

And as you became older
I really began to see
You were a young girl
The splitting image of me

I felt this was a problem
I kind of knew what to expect
An attitude with plenty of secrets
Occasionally lacking respect

But I told you once before
And my words are true
There's nothing in this world
I wouldn't do for you

Battered Woman

As I lay in this bed
All battered and bruised
My face covered in bandages
My heart terribly confused

I'm unable to talk
My mouth is wired shut
My body's in so much pain
My lips are badly cut

I've been given medicine
It seems around the clock
It only numbs the pain
But the sensation doesn't stop

To the world I'm unconscious
But I'm awake in my mind
One day I'll open my eyes
But only in due time

We Need a Resolution

We're still battling this problem
The unanswered question is why
How much more turmoil has to occur
Before another person dies

Although it isn't so simple
However it's very complexed
Many are frustrated with the injustice
And now their feeling vexed

Now videos have been surfacing
Social media has been made aware
Law enforcement is being targeted
Now who's being treated unfair?

Who's the actual victim?
Who is really to blame?
The issue is so problematic
Both sides feel the same

We can't continue to live like this
This conundrum needs to be resolved
Because it'll only becomes worse
As the escalation continues to evolve

Dinner for Two

There are two glasses of wine
On a table that has been set
There's food cooking on the stove
It's not quite finished yet

He keeps checking his watch
He knows it's just about time
The food is almost done
It's almost a quarter to nine

There's a knock at the door
He's nervously surprised
Then he opens the door slowly
And gazes into her eyes

She's about five foot four
And so sexy and fine
With four inch heel stilettos
And a voluptuous behind

He's caught up in the moment
All that he's been through
To ensure everything is perfect
When having dinner for two

Her Time

She gets up early in the morning
In the comfort of her home
To start her morning coffee
And to talk on the phone

She could be often heard
Laughing from time to time
Moving throughout the room
Checking the weather outside

She opens the front door
To allow some sunlight in
She's just finished her coffee
As she's talking to a friend

This is her moment
Some well-deserved time
Where she can be alone
And begin to really unwind

Now that she's relaxed
And in her comfort zone
She's enjoying her time
Just talking on the phone

Not My Type

When an unpleasant situation occurs
We should forgive and forget
I'm still working on that part
But I'm not there just yet

It's easy to overlook the problem
Trust me and believe
When you're not dealing with the issue
The burden is left with me

I keep dealing with this problem
And I'm doing it by myself
Since that appears to be the case
You should find someone else

You're not the man I thought
But I didn't want to believe
You would be such a coward
To pack your clothes and leave

It's easy for you to walk away
And to leave me high and dry
My intuition had already told me
You weren't my type of guy

Based On Your Lies

I've cried far too long
Through all these years
While wasting my time
On these meaningless tears

When I know the truth
And it can't be denied
I have all the proof
I know that you lied

If it was so bad
You should've talked to me
We could've worked it out
But you decided to cheat

I really can't believe
After all that's at stake
You're willing to give up
Our lives over a mistake

I know you know, I'm hurt
And you know you were wrong
Out in the streets lusting
When you had passion at home

Warning Signs

I can't help but to think
About those bad times
In ways my heart has been broken
Through many countless lies

Some of them had fooled me
When others haven't gotten caught
In some of those situations
It definitely wasn't my fault

I know I've overlooked
Plenty of the warning signs
To think this was the one
I gave my heart and mind

But obviously I was wrong
And misled to believe
That somehow you cared
Or truly loved me

I didn't bother to inquire
Or to even ask why
Because I know your response
Would be another lie

As I fight back the agony
Filled with so much pain
I want to return the favor
So you can feel the same

But I'm better than that
There won't be a next time
I've learned from experience
To acknowledge those warning signs

The End

It weeps without knowing
In the most secure place
It usually leaves no clues
Often with no trace

It speaks with no words
And it always chooses sides
Then it suddenly erupts
Each time my heart cries

For the times I carried
This empty burden alone
Waiting for his phone call
But none came through the phone

For all of the disappointments
For the false alibis
For your lying friends
For the unnecessary lies

You never made time for me
But you had time for your friends
That was your major flaw
And the beginning of the end

Every Life Matters

Every person in the world
Has an agenda in life
They attempt to follow a path
That requires some advice

Every life matters
It just happens to be
Something of great worth
That I really, truly believe

People are being shot down
In our neighborhood streets
The fallen outlined in chalk
Being covered with plain sheets

Angered families are outraged
The neighborhood's on alert
Refusing to be the next victim
Lying face down in the dirt

We have choices in this world
And it's our constitutional right
To bear arms and protect
Our neighborhoods and fight

As we come together
It should be no surprise
Our actions are united
As we all continue to rise

Stay True

It's not about the money
It's not about the fame
It's not about the people
Screaming and shouting your name

It's not about the glamour
It's not about the power
It's not about the revenue
Or how much you make an hour

It's about your image
It's about your life
It's about the relationship
You have with your wife

It's about being humble
It's about respect
It's about the hard times
We haven't embraced yet

Please hear my words
Think of what we've been through
Remember the difficult moments
That woman that's been there for you

Military Mothers

When you received your orders
I'd thought I die that day
With my eyes full of tears
I didn't know what to say

I told you I was scared
You said you were too
But you also told me
It was something you had to do

You told me about the others
Received their orders and gone
Just think about their families
Wanting them to come home

Then I began to realize
What you were saying to me
It was your time to deploy
To help keep our country free

I admire your dedication
That's why I look up to you
You have an obligation
You were going to see it through

That day I learned something
Especially about you and me
You're one of the bravest mothers
That's how I want to be

The Game

You've heard it all before
Remember what they said
Allow it to linger around
And ponder inside your head

But don't let it discourage you
The game is still the same
They're just trying to get to you
So please understand the game

They're going to say what they say
They're going do what they do
It's a part of this vicious cycle
That doesn't have any rules

So don't get caught up
You don't need to play
Don't get involved with that
No matter what they say

The Thought Process

A thought is a process
That stimulates the mind
To help formulate an idea
With each and every line

The brain receives the message
As the idea begins to sink
That causes a chain reaction
That requires the brain to think

The thought is being processed
And developed in such a way
The subconscious begins to guide
The mouth on what to say

The words are chosen carefully
And said elegantly with tact
The receiver receives the message
Then responds immediately back

The thought process does work
It's a method of how to think
This tool is very helpful
If utilized before you speak

Freedom

I stand here before you today
To honor Dr. Martin Luther King
For all the sacrifices he made
Because he had a dream

If I could speak to him now
There's a lot I would want to say
Like thank you for your contributions
That has shaped America today

You've broken down many barriers
You've opened our hearts and minds
You emphasized the importance of unity
And to work through those difficult times

You've displayed great compassion
For the rights of all women and men
You've placed your life in danger
Time and time again

When the world was not-so pleasant
Filled with conflict and strife
You continued to strive for equality
While pursuing a better way of life

I imagined Dr. King was baffled
Lying awake late at night
Contemplating with this conundrum
That plagued our human rights

Why wouldn't the world accept?
A person's character or content within
Why should anyone be denounced?
Because the color of their skin

But somewhere in this nation
It seemed America began to believe
A change was on the verge
In 1963

Dr. King didn't have the answer
But he devised a momentous plan
That would change millions of lives
All across this land

I imagined he went into a room
A quiet place somewhere in his home
Where his thoughts began to unravel
As he meditated all alone

He thought about the suffering
The injustice his eyes have seen
All the hatred and the pain
Caused by human beings

He was reminded of a nation
That signed a promissory note
That guaranteed women and men
Their civic right to vote

Dr. King knew it was time
For the world to take a stand
To abolish the chains of discrimination
For every woman and man

Millions gathered from all over
For the entire world to see
One of the largest political rallies
The March on Washington DC

Before Dr. King left the podium
His dream finally came to past
As he looked at the crowd and said
Free at last! Free at last! Thank God Almighty,
We are free at last!

**Kindly use the link below to see video
dedicated especially to Dr. King:**

https://www.youtube.com/watch?v=iJ3Zs5cDa-E

I Thank You

Thank you for reading this book
I hope you enjoyed it too
Maybe you came across something
That really inspired you

Coming from a woman's perspective
Viewing things from her side
It may help others understand
Her reasoning through his eyes

I admit it's kind of complicated
And it's even harder to explain
She's still very reserved
And that'll never change

This book was meant to touch
The center of the reader's soul
It doesn't matter how young you are
Nor it doesn't matter how old

Through these life experiences
She's willing to fight until the end
Her heart has been taken for granted
And mended together again

Her heart bears no shame
And she won't settle for less
All she wants is a better life
And the Lord will do the rest

www.ingramcontent.com/pod-product-compliance
Ingram Content Group UK Ltd.
Pitfield, Milton Keynes, MK11 3LW, UK
UKHW022222230426
12048UKWH00016BA/1006